JOHN RAYN

CW00400847

WALSINGHAM

England's National Shrine of Our Lady

with a Spiritual Reflection
by Peter Rollings

ST PAULS

ST PAULS Publishing
187 Battersea Bridge Road, London SW11 3AS, UK
www.stpaulspublishing.com

A catalogue record is available for this book from the British Library.

Set by Tukan DTP, Stubbington, Fareham, UK
Printed through s|s|media, Wallington, Surrey

ST PAULS is an activity of the priests and brothers
of the Society of St Paul who proclaim the Gospel
through the media of social communication.

Contents

Dedication

*This book is dedicated to Father Noel Wynn
who has been an outstanding
Director of the R.C. National Shrine of
Our Lady of Walsingham.*

Foreword

There are many books about the history of Walsingham and one might be tempted to ask whether another one is necessary. I think that John Rayne-Davis has found a gap in the market and come up with a distinctive offering. He makes the point that royal patronage was the feature that made Walsingham the most important place of pilgrimage in England and goes on to show how all the kings and queens from Henry III to Henry VIII contributed to Walsingham as a place of pilgrimage. In doing so he paints an interesting picture of what England was like in those days. His treatment of the Middle Ages and of the times after the Reformation gives an interesting insight into the place of religion in this country at those times and his vision for the future of the Shrine of Our Lady of Walsingham is worth considering in an England where in his words "materialism has run rampant through society".

I am pleased to recommend this book.

Fr Noel Wynn S.M.
Former Director, R.C. National Shrine, Walsingham

Introduction

Walsingham lies in a beautiful and unspoiled area of North Norfolk. This is an undulating, very rural region, which has a unique character and great charm. One can be forgiven for thinking that time has passed it by, as it appears not to be tainted by the materialism and bustle which are hallmarks of today's society. One finds in Walsingham a quietness and calm which is absent from much of modern life, a quietness and calm that comes from the spiritual heritage of the place.

As one enters the beautiful and very ancient village of Little Walsingham, one detects an almost tangible sense of spirituality which seems to pervade the entire place. This atmosphere doubtless stems from centuries of prayer and devotion to Our Lady, and her son, our Saviour, that has been offered here by the millions of pilgrims who have visited Walsingham since the eleventh century.

Marian devotion has always been central to Catholic spirituality. In Mary we see the first disciple and, *par excellence*, the qualities of obedience, humility, patience, devotion and fortitude. Among her many virtues, she represents caring and nurturing, not only from her years of bringing up the Christ-child, but also from her role, given to her by Christ from the cross, to care for his disciples Through the latter she has become a unique link to God, through her son, for all humanity.

The Church's devotion to Mary was one of the things vigorously opposed by the Protestant reformers in the sixteenth and seventeenth centuries, causing dissension, much suffering and even martyrdom. Even today there is a lack of understanding and mis-representation of what the Blessed Mother of God means to the Catholic community. Prior to the Reformation Walsingham was the focus of Marian devotion in England. Thankfully, due to the combined efforts of both the Catholic and the Anglican Churches since the nineteenth century in re-establish-ing the Shrine, this can be said to be true again today.

Today, we see Walsingham restored to its medieval position as the premier Marian Shrine in the British Isles, although it certainly does not attract the same numbers of pilgrims it did before the Reformation. Each year many hundreds of thousands of people visit both the Roman Catholic National Shrine and the Anglican Shrine, coming not only from all over the United Kingdom, but from all over the world.

Devotion to the Blessed Virgin Mary is a feature of many Shrines throughout the world. These tend to emphasise different aspects of Mary's nature. For instance, Lourdes is dedicated to Mary the healer, whilst Walsingham, because of the way in which it was founded, reflects Mary the Mother of God. Mary's obedience to the call of God at the Annun-ciation enabled the Saviour of the world to be born.

Her maternal care for her child was to be a foretaste of her maternal care for all who followed him. Walsingham, therefore, is a living testimony to this maternal care, witnessed by all who make pilgrimage to this holy place.

A pilgrimage can be a group or an individual activity. Whatever the context, they are highly personal and affect in different ways all who take part. People travel to Walsingham for different reasons and with differing expectations. Many people find that a visit transforms the direction and emphasis of their lives, be it through physical, spiritual or psychological healing. For others it is a time of strengthening or reaffirmation of faith. In this, Walsingham is seen to be a place of renewal, precisely because it is a place where people come very close to the Son of God through devotion to his mother.

Some cynics claim that Walsingham and places like it are nothing but an escape from the harsh reality of the twenty-first century. They might say that Walsingham is purely a bolt hole, or a place for burying one's head in the sand. Nothing could be further from the truth. Walsingham testifies to the one true reality in our lives, namely, that love of God, through Christ, by the intercession of his blessed mother is the centre and purpose of our very existence.

Walsingham can give to the pilgrim a sense of balance, confidence and hope which can greatly restore him or her from the turmoil of today's busy, and often self-centred, world. It is a powerful counter-force to the pressures of modern living where materialism has run rampant through society. It is a place that has affected people's lives deeply for nearly one thousand years and it stands as a powerful symbol of Catholic spirituality. It is truly "England's Nazareth" and a beacon of hope for the future of Christianity in this country.

The Foundation and Development of the Shrine

The Foundation of the Chapel of Walsingham by Richard Pynson, written in verse and commonly called the Pynson Ballad, published c1465, but which may have been written one hundred years earlier, places the foundation of Walsingham during the year 1061. According to this ballad the Shrine at Walsingham came into existence in the following manner. Richeldis de Faverches, the Lady of the Manor of Walsingham Parva (Little Walsingham), a widow and a woman of great wealth, prayed that the Blessed Virgin would allow her to honour her in a special and unique way. For this to happen, Richeldis was transported in spirit to the Holy Land and shown the house in Nazareth in which Mary had grown up and where Mary was told by the angel Gabriel that she would be the mother of God's son.

Mary asked Richeldis to build an exact replica of this holy house in Walsingham for her praise and honour and vowed that all who venerated it would find help. When making her request, it is believed that she said: "Let all who are in any way distressed or in need seek me there in that small house that you maintain for me at Walsingham. To all that seek me there shall be given succour." Richeldis was told to take note of the exact measurements of the house, and during the course of three visions, she memorised the specifications of the building.

Richeldis, anxious to start building, summoned architects and builders to begin construction. Waking one morning, she noticed a nearby meadow was soaked with dew but had two equal sized areas that were left untouched. She interpreted this to be a further message from Our Lady, but was perplexed as to which of these two areas was she supposed to build upon. She decided on the site closest to two wells, but the builders immediately ran into problems and found that nothing appeared to fit together correctly. Eventually they gave up. Richeldis spent the following night praying, entreating Our Lady to come to her aid. In the morning Richeldis saw the building works had moved 200 feet to the second site, and the building was complete. Thus the holy house came into existence through a series of miracles at the hands of the Angels. From its foundation it was known as "The Shrine of Our Lady of Walsingham". A chapel dedicated to St Lawrence was later built on the site.

Some authorities have questioned the date of the foundation of the shrine as being 1061 and believe it may be later than this, their reason being that "de Faverches" is a Norman French name, although the Christian name Richeldis is of Saxon origin. They speculate that Richeldis may have been married to a Norman Knight who accompanied William the Conqueror. Furthermore, they claim that the Domesday Book (1080s) makes no mention of the de

Faverches family owning land at Walsingham. If they are correct in their theory, the date can only be twenty or thirty years out. However, if we go back to the Pynson Ballad it could not be more specific as far as the date of foundation is concerned. It states:

Built the year of Christ's incarnation,
A thousand complete sixty and one
The time of St Edward King of the region.

By the end of the eleventh century and into the two centuries following, the Crusades taking place in the Holy Land prevented people from making pilgrimage to those holy sites. Instead, thousands flocked to Walsingham, thus establishing it as an important centre of pilgrimage and awarding it the title "England's Nazareth" – a title the village holds to this day.

In 1153, Geoffrey de Faverches, who may well have been Richeldis' grandson, arranged for the building of a Priory adjoining the Holy House, to be administered by Augustinian Canons. Some writers, including Elizabeth Obbard have claimed that Geoffrey was Richeldis' son, however this seems very unlikely if one takes into account the short life expectancy in those days. Since the date of the foundation of the shrine was 1061, this would have made Geoffrey more than 90 years old in the 1150s.

Even before the building of the Priory, the chapel of the Holy House received tithes (financial income) from the land it held and this was somewhat unusual. Tithes would more usually be given to the parish church, from which they were distributed. The

Charter for the Priory was confirmed in 1159, with the patrons being Robert de Burgh and Roger, Earl of Clare. In 1169, this same Geoffrey donated the Holy House to the Augustinians on the day he set out on pilgrimage to the Holy Land. Shortly afterwards the Canons enclosed the Holy House within their Lady Chapel and it was at this time that a statue of Mary with the infant Jesus was placed in the Shrine. Today's statue bears a strong similarity to the original, since it is derived from a representation on a medieval seal of the original statue showing the mother and child.

Like its original, today's statue is full of symbolism. The Blessed Virgin is shown crowned in the style of the Saxon period, the crown, used on rare occasions, is made of solid gold and decorated with precious stones. Mary is seated on a throne, which symbolises wisdom. On her lap is the Christ child holding the Gospels, the Good News to the world. His right hand is extended in a double gesture of blessing to the world, and protection towards his mother. Mary holds a three headed lily, the symbol of purity and her virginity. The seven rings on the throne represent the seven sacraments of the Church. The throne is placed upon a "toadstone" (an East Anglian symbol of the devil) which reflects the power of God's goodness to overcome evil.

The popularity of the Shrine grew rapidly and its prosperity escalated, due in part to gifts from pilgrims and legacies, particularly those from the many pilgrims who made arrangements for Masses to be said for their soul after their death. Religious relics, being very much a feature of medieval religious life, were acquired by the Priory and these were venerated with deep devotion by the faithful. The Shrine became adorned with gold and precious stones and this grandeur was in contrast to the unadorned simplicity of the original Holy House erected in the time of Richeldis.

During the thirteenth century Walsingham became a major centre in English life and religious observance. Pilgrims flocked to the Shrine following well defined pilgrim paths across Norfolk, stopping at notable churches or chapels as they went. This brought a higher level of prosperity to the towns and villages on these routes, mainly due to the accommodation, food and drink they supplied to those passing through. In 1485 the Red Mount Chapel at Kings Lynn was built to serve pilgrims on the last leg of their pilgrimage.

The Shrine became one of the four greatest Shrines in the Christian world, the others being Jerusalem, Rome and Compostella, with Walsingham being the only one dedicated to the Mother of God. It was said that the lines of pilgrims walking towards Walsingham in the dark, with their torches burning, were like the stars of the Milky Way in the night sky. This led to people renaming this portion of the sky The Walsingham Way. It is very important to realise that Walsingham, at this time, was even more popular as a Shrine and place of pilgrimage than was Canterbury Cathedral.

The last chapel pilgrims reached before arriving at the Shrine was the Slipper Chapel, standing just over a mile from the Holy House and originally dedicated to St Catherine of Mount Sinai. This dedication to St Catherine is a reminder of the monastery on Mount Sinai, built on the site where Moses saw God in the burning bush, itself a type and prefiguration of the All-holy Theotokos (Mother of God), who bore within her the fire of the Godhead without being consumed. It was at the Slipper Chapel that pilgrims took off their shoes and walked the last mile towards the Shrine barefooted as a sign of contrition and penitence; this became known as The Holy Mile. The Slipper Chapel dates back to 1346 and is one of the very few buildings associated with the Shrine to have survived intact. It probably remained unaffected by the excesses of the dissolution of the Shrine in the sixteenth century because it was too far from the Priory to be associated with it.

By 1486 a lazar-house (so named after Lazarus, the patron saint of lepers) was established in Walsingham and this was endowed in 1491 by Robert Pigut, a local landowner, from his will. This was on the condition that the house took in John Ederich (a leper from Norwich) and his wife and "afterwards to admit two leprous men, or one of good family, from time to time."

In 1511, the Dutch theologian Erasmus visited Walsingham. He described the Shrine and statue of Our Lady as follows:

"When you look in you would say it is the abode of saints, so brilliantly does it shine on all sides with gems, gold and silver... Our Lady stands in the dark at the right side of the altar ... a little image remarkable neither for size, material, or execution."

Erasmus was somewhat cutting in his description of the Shrine. It is known that he favoured changes in the Church and disliked the more ornate aspects of religious symbolism, such as relics. He was also strongly opposed to the excessive wealth many religious houses were acquiring. Erasmus does however mention that there were two wells in a thatched building adjoining the Church, these, to quote an earlier reference to them in the Pynson Ballad, "had the repute of curing headaches and indigestion; and also for the miraculous power of ensuring to the pilgrim whatever wish he might make while drinking the water."

Elsewhere, he describes the chapel of the Virgin or Holy House where the statue of Our Lady stood on the right of the altar, surrounded by gold and jewels as well as testaments provided by pilgrims of the healing powers of Our Lady. The air was perfumed with incense. Each pilgrim prayed before the altar and laid his or her donation there. A priest stood at all times in the Holy House to counsel and pray with pilgrims, as well as to protect the treasures it housed.

Despite Erasmus' criticisms, he recorded a beautiful prayer as he knelt in front of the image of Our Lady:

Oh, alone of all women Mother and Virgin,
Mother most blessed, Virgin most pure,
We salute you; we honour you as best we can
With our humble offerings.
May your Son grant us that,
Imitating your most holy manners, we also

By the Grace of the Holy Ghost
May deserve to conceive the Lord Jesus
Spiritually in our inmost soul, and once conceived,
Never lose Him.

(Prayers of Erasmus collected by Frobenius in 1540)

Archaeological excavations of the site in 1961 revealed many fascinating facts of the original Shrine, amongst them, the chapel was double skinned, with the outer structure made of flint. The windows were originally without glass, although Henry VIII had these glazed, employing Barnard Flower, the Royal glazier, to carry out this work. (It is believed the windows contained scenes showing the history of the Shrine). The most important discovery of them all was the actual measurements of the Holy House itself, 7.11 x 3.91 metres (approx. 23 x 13 feet).

Cardinal Wolsey also visited the Shrine as a pilgrim in 1517 when he was in poor health. He was back in 1520 and appeared to have a true devotion to Our Lady of Walsingham.

History recounts many miracles occurring at Walsingham. In this we turn again to the Pynson Ballad, in which it is claimed that Our Lady performed countless miracles. It states that many conditions of sickness were cured; the dead were restored to life; the disabled were cured and the blind given sight; sailors were saved from shipwreck by intercession to Our Lady of Walsingham. In addition to these, people with mental health problems and lepers were healed, and those people troubled by evil spirits were liberated. The ballad claimed any condition, physical or spiritual, could be cured by "devoutly calling to Our Lady". The miracle of the knight is perhaps among the best known miracle of Walsingham. In this a knight was being pursued near to the Priory, in which he could claim sanctuary. He came to a small door into the grounds, which was closed and, after a prayer for protection to our Lady, he found himself on the other side of the door, still on horseback, and thus escaped from those who were following him. It was claimed that the knight gave his armorial banner to the Shrine in thanks for his deliverance. There was, according to Erasmus, a brass plate describing this miracle in the Priory church. The road to the south side of the Anglican Shrine is still called Knight Street, at the bottom of which can be found a small wooden door leading into the grounds of the Abbey ruins.

In time, corruption crept in to the life of the Shrine, corruption often being a companion to great wealth. One such example involved the rather delightfully named Prior John Snorying. This Prior was accused of financial manipulation, and he was eventually suspended and then removed from office.

There can be little doubt that this corruption was, however, confined in the main to senior clerics – most pilgrims would have been totally unaware that these problems existed. Nor did it overshadow the simple message of the Shrine. Pilgrims continued to flock to the Shrine in their thousands to gain the deep spiritual benefits Walsingham had to offer. However, as we shall see, setting out on pilgrimage during the Middle Ages was not the comfortable journey it is today.

Pilgrimage

In the Middle Ages, as today, pilgrims' motives for taking part in a pilgrimage to Walsingham differed greatly. Some wanted to petition Our Lady for such things as health or material prosperity; others to thank God or one of the saints for a favour granted, such as recovery from an illness or the birth of a child; others were keen to obtain indulgence for remission of their sins; whilst for some it was simply a desire to be closer to the presence of God, which was achieved by getting closer to the mother of his son. During this period of history, those convicted of a criminal offence were often forced to go on pilgrimage to Walsingham as part of the sentence imposed on them by the judicial system of the time.

To go on a pilgrimage was a major undertaking in the Middle Ages. Pilgrims wore distinctive penitential dress, with a cloak made from brown or black material, a broad hat, and carried with them a wooden staff – the means by which they were able to support themselves when tired, or defend themselves when attacked. They also carried with them badges or medals obtained from past pilgrimages – metal, coin-type objects distinctive to the holy site from which they were obtained.

The traditional symbol of a pilgrim at this time

was the scallop shell, used especially by pilgrims on the their way to the Shrine of St James at Santiago de Compostela.

It is important to appreciate the difficulties and dangers of a pilgrimage in the Middle Ages. A pilgrimage would normally begin with Mass, at the end of which the pilgrims would receive a special blessing as they set out on their journey. As they travelled, progress was very slow, as most travelled on foot, although the wealthy sometimes rode on horseback. Roads in medieval England were atrocious, or non-existent and only in towns did one find cobbled streets. In the country, roads were little more than tracks, which became a sea of mud in wet weather. It was quite common to travel only ten to twelve miles in a day, and, if the weather was really bad, it could be much less. There were frequent tolls on the roads and these formed a useful source of income for local landowners; the rates individuals were charged varied according to what it was thought they could afford. By contrast, if, say, a pilgrimage was undertaken from York to Walsingham in medieval times, it would have taken about three weeks to do the journey on foot. Today, this same journey takes about four hours in a comfortable air conditioned coach.

Accommodation on route was extremely basic. Where they could be found, inns were overrun with vermin, many landlords fleeced their guests and provided very poor quality food. There was also a very good chance of getting robbed if staying in an inn. The best accommodation was provided by the network of monasteries and nunneries that spanned the country. Here, at least, people were charged fair prices and received adequate sleeping facilities and nourishing, well cooked food.

There were very real dangers facing the pilgrim as he travelled the country. Much of England was thick forest and in this lurked criminals who targeted pilgrims as victims of robbery or other crimes and this is where the pilgrim staff came into its own as a weapon of defence. Some unwary travellers were murdered. Since their attackers could disappear back into the forest, the chance of them being caught and brought to justice was negligible. It was essential for all the pilgrims to keep together, as any stragglers would be quickly picked off by robbers. As if human dangers were not enough, wild wolves still existed in England and they could easily attack the young or vulnerable, older pilgrims. All pilgrims would have taken a gift to the pilgrimage centre they were visiting and it would have been essential to keep this gift well hidden during their journey. These gifts formed the basis of the wealth of many monasteries and made Walsingham the wealthiest religious house in England.

In the fourteenth century, a catastrophe hit England which was to have a major adverse affect on pilgrimage – the Black Death. The Black Death, or bubonic plague as it is also known, began to sweep across England from Europe. It is thought to have claimed the lives of three million people in England and as many as twenty-five million throughout Europe. It is then not surprising that Walsingham too was affected.

The Augustinian Friars, along with the population of Walsingham, became seriously depleted in number. In 1364, Pope Urban approved measures for the emergency ordination of priests at Walsingham to cope with the ministrations to pilgrims. However, the Black Death had a much more direct effect on pilgrimages. After the end of the first devastating bout, many people became convinced that this scourge was God's punishment for the sins of the world. What better way was there to atone for sin than going on pilgrimage and subjugating oneself in front of Mary the Mother of God?

In John Hatcher's book *The Black Death*: *An Intimate History* he describes an imaginary pilgrimage to Walsingham from a Suffolk village. This pilgrimage was decided upon since the villagers were aware of the spread of the plague through Italy and France and guessed that England would be next on the list. The pilgrims visited Walsingham to gain protection from bubonic plague by the intercession of the Blessed Virgin. There is an extremely intimate description of pilgrims queuing to enter the Holy House, with the pilgrims' reactions described as being "awe at the splendour of the Shrine". It also mentions people selling medals and relics to pilgrims as souvenirs of their visit to Walsingham. Unfortunately, the village in Suffolk did not escape the effects of the plague as it spread northwards throughout England, decimating the population of the country.

The Black Death also caused some cynicism regarding the power of the Church, as many who had survived saw only too clearly that the healing Friars had been unable to cure many people placed in their care. The plague led to extreme, even distorted, religious views and this brought into existence a group of penitents who walked round the country flagellating themselves in public. The plague became a feature of life in England until the eighteenth century. Its arrival in a city, town or village caused panic and many of the wealthier citizens promptly left. It is not surprising therefore that pilgrims on route to Walsingham would have been unwelcome and faced fear and suspicion from the inhabitants of the towns and villages through which they passed.

During the fifteenth century the Wars of the Roses raged from 1455 until 1485. This was a very destructive civil war between two factions of the Plantagenets, The House of Lancaster and The House of York. This long drawn out period of strife caused mayhem in England and would certainly have seriously affected pilgrimages to Walsingham. With armed factions moving up and down the country, it would have been unwise to undertake long journeys. It was quite possible for travellers to be stopped and held captive if they happened to oppose those who were in power in the area being travelled through.

The desire, or need, to undertake a pilgrimage was not, and is not, the reserve of any particular social class of person. Royal patronage was a feature that helped make Walsingham the most important place of pilgrimage in England. Where Kings and Queens went, there nobles followed. The popularity of the Shrine worked its way down the social scale to include working men and women, who were keen to enjoy the spiritual benefits of a pilgrimage to intercede at the feet of the statue of the Blessed Virgin.

Royal Patronage

The popularity of Walsingham grew rapidly after it was visited by King Henry III. In 1226 he visited Bromholm Priory, near Bacton on the Norfolk coast some twenty-five miles from Walsingham, and then moved on to the Shrine. He became a great devotee of Walsingham and certainly visited it on at least four subsequent occasions, giving twenty marks (a mark being the equivalent to two thirds of a pound) towards a golden crown for the statue of Our Lady. In 1251 he gave permission for a fair to be held on the feast of the Blessed Virgin's nativity, and permission for the right to hold a weekly market in the aptly named "Friday Market Place". To help secure the finances of the Shrine, Henry arranged benefactions from different sources, including the Churches of St Peter in Great Walsingham and St Clement's Burnham, which helped put Walsingham on the road to prosperity. His son, Edward I, was to follow his father's example and placed the revenues of seven churches under the direct control of the Priory. Most importantly, Henry passed his love for the Shrine on to his son, Edward.

Edward visited Walsingham on at least twelve occasions. In 1277, before he invaded Wales, he toured East Anglia in order to pray at the Shrines and honour the relics at Walsingham, Bromholm and St Faith's. During another visit, Edward had a near escape from death when a piece of masonry fell from a vaulted roof onto the very spot where he had been sitting playing chess only a few minutes previously. Edward was convinced that he owed his life to the intervention of Our Lady and this strengthened his association with the Shrine.

Edward's son, Edward II, was also greatly devoted to Walsingham and visited it many times. In contrast to his father, he was a weak and vacillating King who alienated many of his nobles. He was however, responsible for founding Kings Hall Cambridge and Oriel College Oxford. He was eventually deposed and forced to abdicate in favour of the child born of his wife, Isabella, and her lover, Mortimer.

Edward III kept up the royal tradition of visiting Walsingham. After he acceded to the throne he had Mortimer executed, and his mother was confined to Castle Rising in Norfolk where he regularly visited her, combining this with a visit to the Shrine at Walsingham. Edward was married to Philippa of Hainault, after whom the Black Lion Inn in Friday Market Place is named – a black lion being the heraldic symbol of her family. The Black Lion Inn is among the oldest buildings in Walsingham.

In 1347 a licence was granted by Pope Clement VI to King Edward for the foundation of a house in Walsingham for Franciscan Friars. This house was under the patronage of Philippa the Countess of Clare, a relative of Prior Thomas Clare. The

Augustinian Priory did all in its power to block what they saw as unfair competition and petitioned Phillipa to change her mind, but she refused. They were principally worried that the Franciscans might offer free accommodation to pilgrims and hence diminish their own revenue. The Countess of Clare, herself a patron of the Shrine, was petitioned by the Augustinians, but to no avail. The Friary opened in 1348 and served pilgrims until it was suppressed, along with the Augustinian Priory, in 1538. The ruins of the Franciscan Priory can be found on the edge of the village facing West on the way to the Catholic Shrine and are now in private ownership. The only remains of the Augustinian Priory, the great east window, stands behind the wall opposite the Anglican Shrine, and this is open to the public.

It is clear that, in the time of Edward III, the fame of Walsingham had spread well beyond England. In 1361 he granted safe conduct to David, King of Scotland, to visit the Shrine on pilgrimage. He also allowed a number of French nobles, held as hostages, to visit Walsingham and even contributed to their expenses. Flemish pilgrims too visited Walsingham during the fourteenth century.

Apart from Royal benefactions there were gifts from the wealthy and the nobility. For instance, in 1381, William of Ufford, 2nd Earl of Suffolk, gave a silver figure of a horse and rider displaying his heraldic emblem, which was offered at the altar of Our Lady of Walsingham.

Royal patronage of Walsingham continued into the fifteenth century, with the monarchs of the day visiting the Shrine. We know that Henry IV's second wife, Joan, came to Walsingham in 1427. In 1469, King Edward IV and his Queen visited, as it is chronicled "As for the King, as I understand he departyd to Walsingham upon Friday come seven-night and the Queen also". As we move into the Tudor era, in common with earlier monarchs, Henry VII displayed his devotion to Walsingham. He stayed in Norwich one Easter and then moved on to the Shrine, "Famous for miracles and made his vows for help and deliverance". Following victory after a battle at Stoke, "he sent his banner to Our Lady of Walsingham where before he made his vows". Henry VII also left an image of silver gilt to be set up at the Shrine.

Henry VIII began his reign with a deep reverence for Walsingham, possibly inspired by being taken there on pilgrimage as a child by his father, Henry VII. In fact in the early part of the reign of Henry VIII, he can probably be said to be one of the English Kings with the greatest devotion to Walsingham of all the monarchs. His first wife, Catherine of Aragon, who was herself very devout, was involved in funding St John's and King's Colleges Cambridge with her Chaplain Bishop John Fisher and often combined visits to them with a pilgrimage to Walsingham. In 1510, only one year after he became King, Henry gave a donation to the Shrine a gold chain and the King's Candle, which was perpetually to burn within the Shrine. A few years later he walked, barefoot, from East Barsham Manor to the chapel of Our Lady, where he gave a very valuable necklace to the Shrine as a gift. This beautiful and ancient manor house still exists, approximately two miles from Walsingham.

In 1513, after the English success at Flodden Field against the Scots, Queen Catherine wrote to Henry "Now go to Our Lady of Walsingham that I have promised so long ago to see". In April of the same year, Henry was informed by Admiral Howard that Arthur Plantagenet (who was under his command), "who being in great peril of shipwreck, called on Our Lady of Walsingham for help and vowed that if it pleased God and her to deliver him, that he would not eat flesh nor fish till he had seen her". The Admiral allowed Arthur Plantagenet time off to visit the Shrine to fulfil his vow.

In the earlier years of Henry's marriage to Catherine of Aragon, she bore him a son, who lived for only a few weeks. Immediately after the child's birth in February 1511, Henry rode to Walsingham, through ice and snow, to give thanks to Our Lady. There is little doubt that Henry was generous in his endowments to the Shrine and each year paid for a candle to burn there constantly, known as "The King's Candle". However, as shall be seen, the reign of Henry VIII proved to be the saddest period in the whole history of the Shrine. By this time, the immense prosperity of Walsingham had moved it away from the original simplicity of when it was founded by Richeldis, and certainly there had been scandals of affluent living and even abuse by the senior clerics and some monks, but the fate that was to befall the Church throughout England, was to have particularly devastating consequences for Walsingham.

The Destruction of the Shrine

Shortly after the break of the Church in England from Rome, Henry introduced the Act of Supremacy. This Act forced all nobles, churchmen and civic dignitaries to swear that supreme power and authority within the church lay with Henry. A large number of them complied straight away, including Richard Vowell (who would prove to be the last Prior of Walsingham) swearing the oath in 1534, with his monks following his example. Vowell's eagerness to comply with the Act possibly indicates his desire to keep in with the establishment so that he was able to protect his own interests via Thomas Cromwell.

Once appointed Lord Chancellor, Cromwell persuaded Henry that his financial problems would be eased if he could acquire the wealth of the monasteries. For Cromwell, this would serve a double purpose, it would enable the King (and himself) to acquire the wealth of the monasteries, but also enable Cromwell to introduce reforms of religious practices which would effectively eradicate Roman Catholicism from England. Cromwell could see that, despite the fact that the monks had nominally accepted the oath of supremacy, they still kept to their former practices.

Cromwell began his campaign by dissolving the

smaller monastic houses, no doubt to whet Henry's appetite for the rich pickings from the larger establishments. As Walsingham was the richest monastic house in England it was clearly top of his hit list. Indeed, Walsingham's wealth was so great that Roger Ascham, the Elizabethan Scholar and writer, remarked that "The Three Kings be not so rich, I believe as was the Lady of Walsingham".

Prior Vowell was a man who had played for time and who, desperate to ingraciate himself with the establishment, was quick to write to Cromwell, sending him huge bribes. One of these was equal to £40,000 in today's money. Vowell's plans paid off and, when the Priory of Walsingham was dissolved, he was given a pension by Cromwell of £100 a year (in excess of £37,000 today). The Canons of the Priory fared less well and received only between £4 – £6 a year.

One of the main people involved in the final death agonies of the Shrine was Sir Richard Southwell. Southwell was a Norfolk man who lived some twenty miles from Walsingham, at Houghton St Faith, close to Norwich. Richard Southwell (the grandfather of St Robert Southwell) was High Sheriff of both Norfolk and Suffolk. He was named with his brother Thomas as a receiver in the Court of Augmentations, which meant they had responsibility for dealing with the lands of dissolved monasteries in East Anglia. It is known that Southwell regularly visited Walsingham in its final years to supervise the winding down of the Shrine on the orders of Henry VIII and was very quick to accept perks for himself, which included "a rich cope and vestment" from Prior Richard Vowell. When Southwell enquired who the cope belonged to, the Prior replied, "For you if it be your pleasure".

During this tumultuous period, discontent inevitably surfaced amongst the people of Walsingham. Some were heard to "express regret that so many houses were dissolved where God was well served and advocating a rising of the commons". George Gysburgh, a local landowner, confessed to plotting with Ralph Rogerson (a lay chorister at Walsingham). He said, "You see how these Abbeys go down and our living goeth away with them; for within a while Binham shall be put down and also Walsingham". He went on to say, "When these men shall come to put down the Abbeys, some men must step up and resist them". Richard Southwell was very quick to write to Cromwell saying that the eleven conspirators should be taken at once and tried. Amongst them was one of the Sub-Priors of Walsingham, Nicholas Mileham. Gysburgh's statement was not a call to start an armed revolt, but talk, in very general terms, of what should happen. However, this had little effect on Southwell and all eleven men were tried at Norwich Castle, found guilty of high treason and condemned to be hanged, drawn and quartered. Nicholas Mileham and George Gysburgh were executed in Walsingham on 28 May 1537. The place of their execution is still called the "Martyrs' Field" and can be found beyond the Orthodox church, which was the old railway station. The other men were martyred at points around East Anglia, no doubt to show to a wider audience the fate of those who plotted against the King and his ministers.

Before the Shrine was surrendered, the ancient statue of Our Lady of Walsingham was taken to London, together with statues from other sites, and they were all burnt in Chelsea. "It was the month of July, the images of Our Lady of Walsingham and Ipswich were brought up to London with all the jewels that hung around them, at the King's commandment, and divers other images, both in England and Wales, that were used for common pilgrimage and they were burnt at Chelsea by my Lord Privy Seal."

Bishop Latimer of Worcester wrote to Cromwell in June 1538 and described the statue in the most derogatory terms possible. In this letter he wrote of the burning of the statue of Our Lady from the Shrine of his own Cathedral of Worcester: "She hath been the Devil's instrument, I fear, to bring many to eternal fire; now she herself with her older sister of Walsingham, her younger sister of Ipswich, and their two sisters of Doncaster and Penrhys will make a jolly muster in Smithfield. They would not be all day in burning."

William Petre, the commissioner appointed by Cromwell to obtain the Priory, alleged it to be riddled with superstition. Southwell made the claim that black magic was being practised by the monks and that he had found evidence of the philosopher's stone on the Priory premises. Finally, on 4 August 1538, Prior Vowell surrendered the Priory and all its contents, including the Holy House which had existed for nearly five hundred years, to Petre. The Priory, together with the Holy House, was burnt to the ground; the jewels, gold and silver, having been appropriated by Henry's commissioner, were sent to Cromwell. Vowell again wrote to Cromwell and tried to get for himself some of the property belonging to the Priory. One must wonder how Henry VIII felt about the destruction of the Shrine, which was a place that had clearly been very special to him in the past. Did he feel any tinge of regret or guilt at this wanton destruction? It is said that on his deathbed he prayed "I bequeath my soul to Our Lady of Walsingham."

In this most tragic manner, ended the beautiful and ancient Shrine of Our Lady of Walsingham, a place that had been an inspiration of hope and faith to millions of pilgrims for centuries. With the demise of Walsingham, a fundamental part of religious fabric of the Catholic Church in England was destroyed and it would take several centuries for it to be reborn.

The Great Sleep

The destruction of the monasteries, perhaps predictably, caused a great deal of resentment among ordinary people. Despite the fact that some monasteries had strayed from the original ideals of their founders, they were popular with the people. Not only were they the source of great spiritual benefits, they also provided many practical and charitable services to the community.

It will come as no surprise to learn that it was impossible to eradicate overnight what Walsingham had represented for centuries before. Devotion to Our Lady of Walsingham had grown over many generations and had become deeply rooted in the lives of the people of England. The ruins were often secretly visited by former pilgrims who recalled happier days and some were punished for their belief in miracles stemming from the Shrine ruins. Sir Roger Townsend, a local magistrate at the time, wrote to Cromwell saying that a poor elderly woman from the nearby town of Wells claimed that a miracle had come about by the statue after its destruction. She was examined by Townsend and punished by way of having a placard with the wording "A reporter of false tales" being placed around her shoulders; she was made to parade about the town on a cold day in

January where she was pelted with snowballs; finally, she was placed in the stocks. Townsend concluded in his letter that: "It shall be a warning to other like persons … I cannot perceive but the said image [statue] is not yet out of some of their heads."

Although there were few, if any, Catholics living in Walsingham and surrounding district, any who visited the ruins would have to disguise their actions. It was noted that the Slipper Chapel, which became a cow shed and an agricultural storage building, had, on occasion, a large, unexplained number of people near it.

Queen Elizabeth I visited Walsingham during the course of one of her "triumphal progresses" around the country. One of the people who accompanied her was Philip Howard, Earl of Arundel, who was subsequently martyred for being a Catholic and later canonised. He wrote a poignant Lament for Walsingham. The last verse of this ballad reads:

Owls do screech where sweetest hymns
Lately were sung,
Toads and serpents hold their dens
Where pilgrims did throng.
Weep, weep O Walsingham
Whose days are nights,
Blessings turned to blasphemies,
Holy deeds to despites.
Sin is where Our Lady sat,
Heaven turned to hell:
Satan sits where Our Lord held sway,
Oh Walsingham farewell.

Following the Reformation in England, Catholicism was declared illegal and anyone discovered practising the faith (including acts of devotion to the Virgin Mary), speaking of it, or found in possession of objects relating to it, would be subject to fines, imprisonment, torture and even execution. The faithful witnessing to the Catholic faith therefore had to be undertaken in clandestine conditions.

During this time the reconversion of England was seen as a high priority for the recently formed religious order called the Jesuits. Many Jesuit priests were sent to England to minister to and support Catholics. Among these hand-picked priests was Robert Southwell the grandson of Richard Southwell, who had much to do with the destruction of Walsingham. Robert Southwell, who was also a noted poet, was eventually captured, tortured and martyred for his faith. He grew up about twenty miles from Walsingham and one may speculate that he may well have visited the ruins as a young man and recalled the Shrine in its heyday.

However, not all of the people of this age were prepared to conform to the prohibition on Marian devotion. Walter Raleigh, the explorer and poet, although from a strongly Protestant family and background, wrote a moving poem in the 1590s which was clearly dedicated to the Mother of God. In this poem he actually mentions Walsingham:

As you came from the holy land
Of Walsingham,
Met you not with my true love
By the way you came?

How shall I know your true love,
That have met many one,
As I went to the holy land
That have come, that have gone?
She is neither white nor brown
But as the heavens fair;
There is none that hath a form so divine
In the earth or air.

During these years of great sleep for Our Lady of Walsingham, life continued in this small market village and it became a legal centre for the area. From 1773 the Quarter Sessions (courts of law constituted to hear less serious offences) were held in the Shire Hall, which had formerly been a building offering accommodation for pilgrims in the days of the Shrine. The Hall, standing at the bottom of the High Street, can still be visited today.

In 1779, a Methodist society had been formed in the village and, in 1781, John Wesley, one of the founders of Methodism, preached in the Methodist chapel in the Friday Market. The present chapel, built in 1791, is one of the oldest Methodist Churches in East Anglia and still exists and functions as a place of worship today. Wesley visited the ruins of the Priory and remarked: "Had there been a grain of virtue or public spirit in Henry VIII, these noble buildings would not have run to ruin".

From the time of its destruction, stones were taken from the ruins of the Priory, some by local land owners for building purposes, others by former pilgrims as souvenirs of what they had treasured and lost; this practice was banned by law at the end of the eighteenth century. Little were they to know that the devastation and destruction before them was not to be the end of the story of Our Lady of Walsingham.

The Rebirth of Walsingham

It was perhaps a question of history repeating itself that the rebirth of Walsingham came about by the actions of a truly pious and very devout woman. Charlotte Boyd, an Anglican, familiar with the history of Walsingham, started legal proceedings in 1894 to purchase the run down Slipper Chapel from Henry Lee Warner, who also owned the ruins of the Abbey at that time. In this same year Charlotte was received into the Catholic Church and five years later she acquired the Slipper Chapel and began its restoration.

She offered the Chapel to Bishop Arthur Riddell of Northampton, which, at that time, was the diocese under which Walsingham came; however, he was not interested and it is reputed that he said to the Cardinal Archbishop: "There are no Catholics in Walsingham". Charlotte then conveyed the Chapel to Downside Abbey, but the Bishop countered this by forbidding the Downside monks to hold services there.

In 1897 a Shrine to Our Lady of Walsingham was restored, by authority of Pope Leo XIII, in the Church of the Annunciation in Kings Lynn, the Catholic parish serving Walsingham. In that same year a statue, approved and blessed by Pope Leo, was placed in the Shrine. During the blessing ceremony, Pope Leo said "When England goes back to

Walsingham, Our Lady will come back to England."

It may come as a surprise that, at first, Walsingham did not gain much acceptance from Catholics after the restoration of the Slipper Chapel. Many saw pilgrimage centres as something associated with the continent, and the ancient recusant families went as far as to brand this new Shrine as "un-English". This apparent lack of enthusiasm may have stemmed from centuries of persecution and fear of openly witnessing to the Catholic faith, and it has to be remembered that the Catholic hierarchy had been restored only in 1850, not much more than a generation ago. However, pilgrimages were re-vived in 1897 when the Guild of Our Lady of Ransom, dedicated to the restoration of England as the Dowry of Mary to bring England back to the Catholic Faith, held the first post-Reformation pilgrimage to Walsingham, which was attended by Charlotte Boyd.

The debt owed to Charlotte Boyd for her work to bring pilgrimage back to Walsingham should be acknowledged as one of the great moments in the history of the Shrine. Unfortunately, she never lived to see the full rebirth of Walsingham, as she died in 1906. Perhaps one day her body, which is presently in St Mary's Cemetery, Kensal Green, might one day be laid to rest beside the Slipper Chapel which she restored to Catholic ownership and hence paved the way for the National Shrine as we know it today.

In the early years of the twentieth century the Catholic population in the area increased and a small Catholic church, which had a stained glass window of Our Lady of Walsingham, was opened at nearby Fakenham. In 1933, Laurence William Youens was appointed Bishop of Northampton and he became determined that Walsingham rather than Kings Lynn should become the Roman Catholic National Shrine of our Lady. The Slipper Chapel was brought under the jurisdiction of the Diocese and the Chapel refurbished. In 1934 Cardinal Bourne, Archbishop of Westminster, led a pilgrimage to Walsingham, attended by 10,000 Catholics. During this pilgrimage, Benediction was celebrated in the Slipper Chapel and from that time on the Slipper Chapel officially became the National Shrine to Our Lady in England.

In 1935 the first resident priest was appointed to administer the Shrine and three years later the Holy Ghost Chapel, which adjoins the Slipper Chapel, was built and consecrated by the then Bishop of Northampton, Lawrence Youens. Also in 1938 a very well attended Catholic Youth pilgrimage to Walsingham was led by Cardinal Hinsley, Archbishop of Westminster.

After the Second World War the story of the rebirth of Walsingham continued at a considerable pace, some of the highlights of which were a cross-carrying pilgrimage of peace in 1948, for which teams of people carried a total of fourteen crosses from different parts of the country to Walsingham. Upon their arrival in Walsingham on 16th July Cardinal Griffin consecrated England and Wales to the Immaculate Heart of Mary. The text of his homily can be found in the Appendix. These pilgrim crosses are today arranged as the Stations of the Cross adjoining the Chapel of Our Lady of Reconciliation. In 1950, a temporary Church of the Annunciation was built next to Elmham House in the village to serve the needs of Catholics living in Walsingham as well as pilgrims staying there. In 1953, the "Assumption window" was placed in the Slipper Chapel. In 1954, Archbishop O'Hara crowned the statue of Our Lady of Walsingham. In 1961, excavations revealed the position of the original Holy House which was destroyed in the Reformation. They also showed a larger chapel, built to enclose it, just north of the nave. This is a short distance to the west of the remaining east window arch, the only visible remains of the original Priory, and a small wooden plaque set into the grass now marks the spot of this discovery. During the excavations, evidence of burning was found, which confirms the contemporary accounts of its destruction. These discoveries were made exactly nine hundred years after the foundation of the Shrine by Richeldis. In this same year the ancient and beautiful Anglican parish church of St Mary's Walsingham was devastated by fire.

Other notable events include the Marist Fathers taking over responsibility for the Shrine in 1968; work they still undertake today. Diocesan boundary changes within the Catholic Church brought into existence the Diocese of East Anglia in 1976, when hardly surprisingly, Walsingham became a pivotal focus within this new Diocese. In 1980, an act of reconciliation and friendship was undertaken when the Archbishop of Canterbury, Dr Robert Runcie, went to the Slipper Chapel and prayed for Christian unity. This gesture did much to remove the centuries of discord between the Catholic and Anglican Church. A few weeks earlier Cardinal Basil Hume, the Archbishop of Westminster, had visited the Anglican Shrine and offered prayers for unity and harmony.

In September 1980 work started on the beautiful and very spacious Chapel of Our Lady of Reconciliation at the Catholic Shrine. This building, shaped like a Norfolk barn, has moveable doors behind the altar so that it can used for open air Masses. The altar, originally in an open-air sanctuary, contains the relics of St Laurence of Rome (martyred 258), St Thomas Becket (martyred 1170) and St Thomas More (martyred 1535). The Chapel was completed in 1982 and consecrated on 22 May 1982 by Bishop Alan Clark, the Bishop of East Anglia. At the time of its consecration, Cardinal Basil Hume said, "The spirituality of this Chapel is in its title."

In May 1982 Pope John Paul II visited the United Kingdom and the statue of Our Lady of Walsingham was taken to the open air Mass at Wembley Stadium, attended by 80,000 people and, at the Pope's request, the statue was placed upon the altar at which he said Mass. The Pope venerated this statue and referred to the Shrine at Walsingham when he said: "Let us learn this from Mary our Mother. In England, 'the Dowry of Mary', the faithful, for centuries have made pilgrimage to her Shrine at Walsingham. Today Walsingham comes to Wembley, and the statue of Our Lady of Walsingham, present here, lifts our minds to meditate on our Mother."

In 1986, Elmham House (formerly the home of Walsingham Grammar School, established in 1639) was extended to provide additional accommodation and amenities for visitors. In 1994 two annexed buildings were purchased and are now called St Anne's and St Joseph's, offering en suite accommodation and a Common Room capable of seating sixty people.

In 1996, The Anglican Bishop of Norwich prayed at the Slipper Chapel during a pilgrimage to celebrate 900 years of Christianity in East Anglia. In 2007, the Catholic church of the Annunciation in the village was replaced by a church which must rate very highly architecturally as one the most attractive modern Catholic churches in existence. This building has the added benefit of being powered by solar panels and geothermal energy. It was consecrated by Bishop Michael Evans of East Anglia on the Feast of the Annunciation 2007. The relics of St Felix and St Constantia (first-century martyrs) from the altar stone of the old church were included in the new altar stone along with those of St Thérèse of Lisicux, St Peter Chanel and St Marcel Champagnat.

It is not only the Catholic Church that has been responsible for restoring pilgrimages and devotion to Our Lady of Walsingham, the Church of England had also played a very significant part. In 1921, the Revd Alfred Hope Patten was appointed Vicar of the Anglican parish church in Walsingham and his devotion to Our Lady prompted him to build a Shrine. Work began in 1930 on a site across the road from where the Priory once stood and there were exciting developments when a spring was uncovered, like that which existed in the original Priory. Water from this spring is regularly used today during services in the Anglican Shrine.

At the centre of the Anglican Shrine stands a replica of Richeldis' Holy House, built to the known specifications of the original Holy House. Contained within its walls are stones from many pre-Reformation abbeys and churches in England, placed there as a sign of reparation for the destruction, as well as stones from other international places of pilgrimage. It is important to acknowledge that the Anglican contribution to restoring Walsingham as a centre of pilgrimage is immense and on-going. The Revd Colin Stephenson, who succeeded Hope Patten as the Administrator of the Anglican Shrine, wrote of an interesting discovery – in former times pilgrims would carry home with them lead bottles, emblazoned with a crowned *W*, known as ampullae, containing the healing waters of Walsingham. In 1967 one of these containers was washed up on the Yorkshire coast from where it is believed it may have been lost overboard by returning pilgrims in the Middle Ages. When discovered, the bottle was sealed, but when opened the remaining liquid inside smelled faintly of roses.

The Future of Walsingham

Some people may claim there is a clear anomaly in having two Shrines with the same dedication within the one village. It is, however, history that has brought about this situation, and it is an unfortunate reminder that the Christian Church remains divided. This is highlighted not only by the presence of the Anglican and Catholic Shrines, but there is also a Russian Orthodox Chapel in the village, and the Methodist Church in which Wesley preached is still thriving.

Many pilgrims to Walsingham do visit both Shrines and derive great spiritual benefit from doing so. Organised annual pilgrimages can draw in thousands at a time. These include the May National Pilgrimage organised by the Anglican Shrine; The Dowry of Mary Pilgrimage to the Catholic Shrine, which is a truly international event with seventeen ethnic chaplaincies represented. Many Catholic dioceses have an annual pilgrimage and many Religious Orders, Pro-Life Groups and groups such as Divine Mercy, Day with Mary and Padre Pio groups come regularly. The New Dawn Catholic Charismatic Conference, Youth 2000 Catholic Youth Festival and the Anglican Youth Pilgrimage are all held during the summer months, which rightly encourages those who are the future of the church; as well as the many diocesan and parish pilgrimages from around the country. Walsingham also draws in visitors from around the world, notably the USA and Australia, and from other religions, particularly Muslims, who revere both Mary and Jesus. To help promote devotion to Our Lady of Walsingham there are in existence a number of societies linked to one or other of the Shrines, these include the predominantly Catholic Walsingham Association, the Anglican Society of Our Lady of Walsingham and the Priests Associate of the Holy House.

One of the prime objectives of Walsingham is to pray for reconciliation, not just of the individual but to bring together conflicts and divisions in the families, communities, churches and nations to which we belong. Whilst no-one could dispute the terrible events that ended the Shrine in 1538, they are now history and the future has to be about building bridges between peoples and not dwelling on past divisions.

Recently in Walsingham, a small group of Roman Catholics and Anglicans joined together for a Pilgrimage of Reparation. They came together to pray at various sites in Walsingham to make Reparation for the sins of the past. How profound it was for them to witness Anglicans leading prayers of reparation for the tragedy of the Reformation. At the beginning of the pilgrimage in East Barsham, at the All Saints Anglican Church, they renounced greed, hatred and fear, as well as the violence done in the name of Jesus who came to bring life, forgiveness, healing and wholeness. There was need to apologise to each other, for apology creates a climate for listening to our wounded past and opens up the possibility for positive reconciliation and healing. Reconciliation can never come about by glossing over wrongs. Of this, Pope John XXIII said, "Responsibility is laid upon us all; we will not try to discover who was right and who was wrong." We must seek the Truth above everything and one of the best practical rules is that we must never forget to make prayers a priority and then to get to know each other better. We can take our work for unity seriously only when the divisions between us give us pain. We can all pray and ask forgiveness for where we as a Church have failed to live the Word of God, been arrogant and unloving.

The Pilgrimage continued with prayers of reparation before a broken altar stone, a litany of reparation to the Blessed Sacrament, prayers of reparation for the sacrilege of graves in the churchyard. The people then moved to the ancient Priory ruins and had various poignant prayers at the site of the high altar, the ancient shrine and at the wells. They prayed in sorrow for the destruction in Chelsea of the statue of Our Lady of Walsingham and then moved on to building in the High Street, underneath which is a small cellar where the two men of Walsingham, George Gisborough and Nicholas Myleham, the sub Prior of Walsingham Priory, were held overnight before they were put to death in the Martyrs' Field. The cellar was furnished as a chapel but the building is currently (2010) inaccessible to the public. The Pilgrimage of Reparation finished at the Martyrs'

Field where the participants prayed and remembered the sacrifice and heroic faith of the sub prior of Walsingham and the many like him who died for the Faith in this land – and so ended a powerful day of prayer in Walsingham.

In the words of Fr Gilbert OFM Cap, one of the last Franciscans to live in Walsingham, "It is for this overwhelming favour of the grace for England to return to Christ and His Blessed Mother, rather than for merely individual and personal favours, that pilgrims tread once more the Walsingham Way."

If Christianity is to survive in this country, places like Walsingham, which have real religious significance, will assume a vital role in nurturing those trying to find meaning in their lives. Walsingham offers a true alternative to the very superficial and ever-shifting aspirations of society today. It shows, in a very tangible way, the importance of the Christian belief in the life, teachings, death and resurrection of Our Lord and the example of his Blessed Mother and not the past machinations of clerics and monarchs. Walsingham could well be one of the keys to spiritual revival in England and, if this proves to be the case, it will grow massively in importance. This would certainly be in keeping with the purpose of the original Shrine and the actions of Richeldis in 1061 when she first encountered the Blessed Virgin.

"The Blessed Virgin is a means between the great clearness of the sun and the horrid darkness of night" (St John Fisher).

A pilgrim emblem

The seal of Walsingham Priory

An artist's drawing of Walsingham Priory

The remains of the Priory east window

The temporary Catholic Parish Church of the Annunciation

The Anglican Parish Church of St Mary

The Anglican Shrine Church

The Holy House in the Anglican Shrine

The first Catholic pilgrimage to Walsingham since the Reformation 19th August 1934 © Universe Archives

The Slipper Chapel

The interior of the Chapel of Reconciliation

The Methodist Chapel

The Orthodox Chapel

A present day pilgrimage to Walsingham

The Catholic Parish Church of the Annunciation

Spiritual Reflection

by Peter Rollings

Pilgrims to Walsingham will often ask, "Where did Our Lady appear?" and are disappointed or puzzled to be told that there has never been any claim to an appearance of the Blessed Virgin at Walsingham.

Walsingham is unique among the major Marian Shrines in that it is not based on a vision of Our Lady or centred on a celebrated image. It has its origin – according to the account given in the Pynson Ballad – in a dream of the lady Richelis de Faverche. There are good scriptural precedents for this. In the Book of Genesis, Jacob had a dream in which he saw the ladder reaching up into heaven. "How awesome is this place. This is none other than the House of God and the Gate of Heaven." He named the place Bethel – House of God. The patriarch Joseph had his dreams. The prophet Daniel gazed into the visions of the night. In St Matthew's Gospel, St Joseph was instructed in a dream to take Mary to his home as his wife. In Richeldis' dream she was taken in spirit to the Holy Land where Our Lady showed her the house where the Annunciation took place and she was instructed to take careful note of its measurements and to build a replica of it at Walsingham.This Holy House was at the centre of the Walsingham devotion.

It was not the house of the Holy Family where Jesus grew up but the house of Joachim and Anne, Mary's parental home. The gospel is clear that, after the Annunciation, Joseph took Mary to his own home so that before this she was obviously in the house of her parents. This is important for a right understanding of the spirituality of Walsingham. When people think of the Holy House of Nazareth they automatically think of the Holy Family but Walsingham's Holy House is a different Holy House. It is not about the Holy Family, it is about the place of the Annunciation, a much deeper and richer idea but at the same time a more difficult concept.

When Erasmus visited the Shrine in 1519 he left a description in which he said the Holy House contained an altar and an image and many votive offerings. He said it was so rich that you would think you were in the mansions of the saints. But originally it would have been completely empty. If you want a good impression of what this would have been like, go to West Stow near Bury St Edmund's where an Anglo Saxon village has been recreated. There you will find a house almost exactly like the one Richeldis made, a simple construction of wood and thatch. When you go into its dim interior you find yourself imagining what it would have been like to live there. Pilgrims came to the small wooden house that Richeldis had built to contemplate the great joy of the angelic salutation, "the ground and original root of mankind's gracious redemption" as the Pynson Ballad says. The emptiness, the space, is essential to the meaning of Walsingham.

When the Romans sacked Jerusalem in 70AD, they

entered the Holy of Holies in the Temple expecting to find great treasure but were astonished to find an empty room. True, it had once contained the Ark of the Covenant but by this time it had long been lost. The meaning of the Holy of Holies was that it was the dwelling place of God, the place where God and man came face to face, an encounter that could not be represented by anything that the human mind could devise. In the New Covenant Mary's womb becomes the Holy of Holies, where the Word of God becomes flesh and dwells with men. This empty space becomes the place of the new creation where God makes all things out of nothing. "He has regarded his handmaiden in her nothingness" sings Mary in her *Magnificat*. The emptiness, the space of the Holy House, reflects this. Walsingham is about making space for God. It is about being receptive to the Holy Spirit. Before we can be filled with the Spirit we have to be emptied. Saint Paul tells us that Christ Jesus "did not cling to his equality with God but emptied himself to assume the condition of a slave and became as men are." Because the Second Person of the Blessed Trinity emptied himself, the Incarnation was able to take place. Because Mary made space for God, he was able to fill her womb. The Holy House of Walsingham is the place of the Incarnation.

In Bethlehem, in the Grotto of the Nativity, the famous silver star marking the place of Our Lord's birth has an inscription: "Here Jesus Christ was born of the Virgin Mary." At Nazareth a similar marker beneath the altar in the place of the Annunciation says "Here the Word was made Flesh." Nazareth is the place of the greater miracle.

Because of the presence of the Holy House, Walsingham is England's Nazareth. Saint Aelred of Rievaulx, the great twelfth-century English saint, reflecting on the name Nazareth as meaning "City of Flowers", said "Nazareth, where the Scriptures flower." *(S. Aelred: Treatise on Jesus at Twelve Years Old.)*

Walsingham, too, is a place where the Scriptures can flower through deep reflection on the Word of God. In the statue of Our Lady of Walsingham the Word of God is central. At the heart of the figure is the Book of the Gospels held by Jesus, the Word made Flesh, who himself is held by Mary, the Seat of Wisdom. Many other Marian Shrines have particular devotions and practices. When you come to Walsingham there is nothing special that you must do. It is a place for contemplation, for reflection, for listening. The original inspiration was that it would be a perpetual reminder of the great joy of the Annunciation. As Aelred said of the Annunciation: "All the joy, all the hope, all the liberty that is ours began this day" *(S. Aelred: Sermon on the Annunciation)*. Standing in the Holy House, the Walsingham pilgrim of old was meant to be filled with a deep sense of joy and wonder at what God has done for us and be led to a deeper understanding of the Word of God. The modern pilgrim, in the presence of the Blessed Sacrament in the Slipper Chapel or in the Holy House of the Anglican Shrine, has the same experience.

Another feature of the Walsingham devotion is that it is all God's work. In the Pynson Ballad account of the founding of the Shrine we hear how the carpenters summoned by Richeldis were unable to complete their task and how, after Richeldis had spent the night in prayer, the Holy House was found to be complete. As the Psalm says, "Unless the Lord build the house, in vain do the builders labour." Just as God built himself a dwelling in the womb of the Virgin Mary who placed herself at the service of his plan, so, when we abandon ourselves to his will does he build us up. This is something which has been experienced again and again at Walsingham.

This is a place of miracles. There has never been much emphasis on the miracles at the Shrine and most of them are unrecorded but there is one which happens time and time again. It is the gift of Faith. So many people have come to Walsingham not knowing what they believe or not knowing what God is asking of them and they go away with full hearts. The experience of Bruno Scott James, who was to become the first Priest Custodian of the restored Shrine, is typical. In his autobiography *Asking for Trouble* he gives a moving account of how, while still an Anglican, he was in the depths of despair about his future and where God wanted him to be. He walked out to the Slipper Chapel and obtained the key from the custodian. (The chapel had not yet been restored as the National Shrine.) Inside, he threw himself to the floor and placed his life in God's hands. From that moment he knew exactly what he must do. On another occasion an American lady who had no particular faith had come to the Slipper Chapel simply because there was a coach trip from the Base at Mildenhall and she was a busy and stressed mother who needed a day out. She set foot inside the Chapel and was converted on the spot. Full of excitement she ran out and cannoned into Father Roland Connelly blurting out, "Father, I'm a Catholic!" to which he replied, "So am I."

It is not surprising that the gift of Faith should be so prominent here because Mary's response to the Annunciation was faith. "*Fiat.*" "Let it be done to me according to your word."

Seeking God in prayer, making ourselves available to him, putting our resources at his disposal, cooperating with his will and work: all these are elements of the Annunciation and of the Walsingham story. The story continues to unfold. It is 950 years since Richeldis was inspired to found the Holy House and in that time the Shrine has developed in different ways. It has had its Joyful Mysteries of growth, its Sorrowful Mysteries of dissolution and decay and its Glorious Mysteries of renewal are now with us. In the last 75 years since the Slipper Chapel became the focus for Catholic devotion there has been great development. At first, the emphasis seemed to be on reparation and restoration. In the 1970s there was a growth of diocesan and parish pilgrimages as the Shrine played its part in the renewal that came from the Second Vatican Council. At the present time there is a sense in which Walsingham is reflecting the great diversity of the Church in England.

Pope John Paul II once said that the heart of a

nation beats in its National Shrine. There is a truth in this. If Walsingham is the place of the Incarnation then all the joys, sorrows and hopes of the people of God will become incarnate here. Walsingham will continue to be a reflection of the Church in this land and all will find a home here. Because in one sense there is nothing special about the Walsingham devotion it can be a home to all. Bishop Alan Clark was once asked by a pilgrim if he thought Our Lady of Walsingham would mind if they carried a statue of Our Lady of Fatima along the Holy Mile. His reply was "I'm going to Lourdes next week, I'll ask her!" There is no competition between devotions. So today, you will find Divine Mercy pilgrimages, Padre Pio groups, Fatima pilgrims, Tamil pilgrimages including Sikhs, Muslims and Hindus, charismatic renewal weeks, ordinary parish groups and great diocesan days and, day by day, the continuing stream of individuals who are drawn by the holiness of this place. The essence of Walsingham is pure Gospel: "The Word was made flesh and lived among us" and this good news is for everyone.

Walsingham has a future part to play in the evangelisation of England. Pope Leo XIII, when restoring the Shrine of Our Lady of Walsingham in 1897, prophesied that "When England returns to Walsingham, Our Lady will return to England." We have the proud boast that we are the Dowry of Mary, a claim which no other country has dared to make. If we are to be the special gift which the Father has given to Mary then we need to work hard to be worthy of that privilege. Walsingham has a very important part to play in bringing the holiness which is the vocation of every Christian into every part of the country. Pilgrims come to Walsingham to be renewed in their faith and to take back to their homes and parishes something of what they have experienced here. Every home can be a Holy House where space is made for God. Every parish can be a Walsingham where Mary points us to her Son, the Word of Life.

Appendix

Pynson Ballad

Of this chapel see here the foundation
Builded the year of Christ's incarnation
A thousand complete sixty and one
The time of Saint Edward king of this region.
Behold and see ye ghostly folks all
Which to this place have devotion
When ye to our Lady asking succour call
Desiring here her help in your tribulation
Of this her chapel ye may see the foundation
If ye will this table oversee and read
How by miracle it was founded indeed.
A noble widow sometime lady of this town
Called Rychold in living full virtuous
Desired of our Lady a petition
Her to honour with some work bounteous
This blessed virgin and lady most gracious
Granted her petition as I shall after tell
Unto her worship to edify this chapel.
In spirit our Lady to Nazareth her led
And showed her the place where Gabriel her grette
Lo daughter consider to her our Lady said
Of this place take thou surely the mette
Another like this at Walsingham thou set
Unto my laud and singular honour
All that me seek there shall find succour.

Where shall be had in a memorial
The great joy of my salutation
First of my joys ground and original
Root of mankind's gracious redemption
When Gabriel gave to me relation
To be a mother through humility
And God's son conceive in virginity.
This vision showed thrice to this devout woman
In mind well she marked length and brede
She was full glad and thanked our Lady then
Of her great grace never destitute in need
This foresaid house she thought to speed
Called to her artificers full wise
This chapel to forge as our Lady did devise.
All this a meadow wet with drops celestial
And with silver dew sent from on high adown
Except the twain places chosen above all
Where neither moisture nor dew might be found
This was the first prognostication
How this our new Nazareth here should stand
Builded like the first in the Holy Land.
When it was all formed then had she great doubt
Where it should be set and in what manner place
Inasmuch twain places were found out
Tokened with miracle of our Lady's grace
That is to say twain quadrates of equal space
As the fleece of Gideon in the wet being dry
Assigned by miracle of holy maid Mary.
The widow thought it most likely of congruence
This house on the first soil to build and arear
Of this who list to have experience
A chapel of Saint Lawrence standeth now there

Fast by twain wells experience doth lere
There she thought to have set this chapel
Which was begun by our Lady's counsel.
The carpenters began to set the fundament
This heavenly house to arear up on high
But soon their works showed inconvenient
For no piece with other would agree with geometry
Then were they all sorry and full of agony
That they could not ken neither measure nor mark
To join together their own proper work.
They went to rest and laid all things on side
As they on their mistress had a commandment
She thought that our Lady that first was her guide
Would convey this work after her own intent
Her men to rest as for that night she sent
And prayed our Lady with devout exclamation.
And as she had begun to perform that habitation.
All night the widow remained in this prayer
Our blessed Lady with heavenly ministries
Herself being here chief artificer
Areared this said house with angels' hands
And not only reared it but set it there it is
That is two hundred foot and more in distance
From the first place books make remembrance.
Early when the artificers came to their travail
Of this said chapel to have made an end
They found each part conjoined sand fail
Better than they could conceive it in mind
Thus each man home again did wynde
And this holy matron thanked our Lady
Of her great grace showed here specially.
And sith here our Lady hath shewed many miracle

Innumerable now here for to express
To such as visit this her habitacle
Ever like new to them that call her in distress
Four hundred year and more the chronicle to witness
Hath endured this notable pilgrimage
Where grace is daily showed to men of every age.
Many sick been here cured by our Lady's might
Dead again revived of this is no doubt
Lame made whole and blind restored to sight
Mariners vexed with tempest safe to port brought
Deaf wound and lunatic that hither have fought
And also lepers here recovered have be
By our Lady's grace of their infirmity.
Folk that of fiends have had encumbrance
And of wicked spirits also much vexation
Here be delivered from every such chance
And souls greatly vexed with ghostly temptation
Lo here the chief solace against all tribulation
To all that be sick bodily or ghostly
Calling to our Lady devoutly.
Therefore every pilgrim give your attendance
Our Lady here to serve with humble affection
Yourself ye apply to do her pleasance
Remembering the great joy of her annunciation
Therewith conceiving this brief compilation
Though it halt in metre and eloquence
It is here written to do her reverence.
All lettered that will have more intelligence
Of the foundation of this chapel here
If ye will ask books shall you enhance
More clearly to understand this foresaid matter
To you shall declare this chronicler

All circumstance by a nobel process
How old chroniclers of this bear witness.
O England great cause thou hast glad for to be
Compared to the land of promise Sion
Thou attainest by grace to stand in that degree
Through this glorious Lady's supportation
To be called in every realm and region
The Holy Land Our Lady's Dowry
Thus art thou named of old antiquity.
And this is the cause as it appeareth by likeness
In thee is builded new Nazareth a mansion
To thy honour of the heavenly empress
And of her most glorious salutation
When Gabriel said at old Nazareth ave
This joy here daily remembered for to be.
O gracious lady glory of Jerusalem
Cypress of Sion and joy of Israel
Rose of Jericho and star of Bethlehem
O glorious lady our asking not repel
In mercy all women ever thou dost excel
Therefore blessed lady grant thou thy great grace
To all that thee devoutly visit in this place.
Amen.

Priors of Walsingham

Ralph	1153	Simon de Wineton	1335
Richard	1173	Thomas Clare	1349
Alexander	1186	John Snoring	1359
William	1207	John Harford	1387
Peter	1254	Hugh Wells	1402
Alanc.	1263	Thomas Hunt	1437
William	1270	John Farewell	1474
John	1279	William Lowth	1503
Philip	1299	Richard Vowell	1514
Walter de Wyghtone	1313		

Administrators of the Catholic Shrine

Canons Regular of St Augustine	1150 – 1538
Benedictine Monks of Downside	1897 – 1930
Diocese of Northampton	1930 – 1934
Bruno Scott James, Priest Custodian	1934 – 1942
Arthur Brewer	1943 – 1944
(Assisted by Capuchin Friars)	1937 – 1948
Gerard Roberts, Priest in Charge	1944 – 1948
Gerard Langley, Priest in Charge	1948 – 1949
Gerard Roberts, Priest in Charge	1949 – 1951
Gerard Hulme, Priest in Charge	1951 – 1968
Roland Connelly S.M., Administrator	1968 – 1978
Sr Kathleen Moran, Pro-Administrator	1978 – 1979
Clive Birch S.M., Director	1979 – 1984

Peter Allen S.M., Director	1985 – 1992
Alan Williams S.M., Director	1993 – 2000
Noel Wynn S.M., Director	2001 – 2009
Alan Williams S.M., Director	2009 –

Administrators of the Anglican Shrine

Alfred Hope Patten	1931
John Colin Stephenson	1958
Charles David Smith	1968
Alan Vincent Carefull	1973
Christopher George Colven	1981
Roy Fellows	1987
Martin Clive Warner	1993
Philip John North	2002
Lindsay Goodall Urwin	2009

The Address given by Cardinal Griffin
on the occasion of
the Consecration of England and Wales
to the Immaculate Heart of Mary,
Walsingham 16 July 1948

'But there is no way of casting out such spirits as this except by prayer and fasting.' (Mt 17:20)

It is a great joy to me to meet you here in your thousands at this time-honoured Shrine of Our Lady for what is, in truth, a very solemn occasion.

Today, at the request of the Archbishops and Bishops of England and Wales, I am to dedicate this country to the Immaculate Heart of Mary. This is, in itself, a glorious event, but if the vast majority of you have travelled here today to show your love and devotion to Our Lady, there are some amongst you for whom today is but the culmination of a pilgrimage which has been spread over the past fortnight. For the last fourteen days, through the towns and villages of this land, along highways and through country roads, you have been approaching this Shrine, bearing with you a cross as the emblem of Christ's triumph over the world and the materialistic conditions in which we live. Some of you have come from Canterbury, from the scene of many pilgrimages in the past. Others have come from Westminster Cathedral, travelling from the great metropolis to this little village in Norfolk. Others have come on foot well over two hundred miles from Wales and from the west. More still from the Peaks and the industrial centres of the north. All have been converging on this spot for this solemn act shortly to be performed. From all sides we have learned of the enthusiasm with which these little bands have been greeted. We have read of those wonderful scenes where you have set up your crosses, recited the rosary and where the word of God has been preached. Fourteen days, travelling on foot, is in truth a pilgrimage. But not merely that, it is an act of penance and prayer. I know that it is with this in mind that you have given up your short and well-earned holidays to perform this act of devotion. I congratulate you and thank you for what you have done. Your pilgrimage has been a source of inspirations to thousands, Catholic and non-Catholic, many of whom would have wished to make the journey with you and all of whom have been very much with you in spirit. Not from this country alone have you come, for a party of French students have come from Boulogne, bringing with them a statue of their own patron, Our Lady of Boulogne. For Our Lady stands above the nations of the world. She is the mother of Christ, given to the world as our mother by her divine Son as he hung upon the cross.

And so today we are happy to welcome so many thousands of Catholic mothers who have come here in the same spirit of prayer and penance. You have travelled many miles and some of you have been travelling all night. May our divine Lord and His holy mother bring a blessing on your families and the families of the nation for whom you have performed this act of devotion.

Whilst we are paying our respects to Our Lady of Walsingham and dedicating ourselves and the country to the Immaculate Heart of Mary we must also think of Fatima. On the 13th May, twenty-one years ago, at the very time of the communist revolution in Russia, Our Lady chose to appear at Fatima to three little children. On this, and on succeeding occasions when she appeared, she insisted upon the recitation of the rosary. She insisted on prayer and penance as the answer to the evils in the world today. Pilgrimages were to be made to Fatima and, indeed, thousands travel there each year. But pilgrimages, for all their outward show of devotion to the mother of God, are but the symbols of that ever-living love with which our daily lives must be filled. We have to carry that same spirit of prayer and penance into our ordinary daily lives, into the affairs of each day, no matter what their outward importance. Prayer, then, and penance, is the answer to the materialism with which we are surrounded today. This was Our Lord's solution to the problems of His day. Do you remember when the apostles, having failed to cast out an evil spirit in a boy, asked Our Lord what was the cause of their failure? He urged them to faith, and then explained that there is no way of casting out such spirits as this except by prayer and fasting.

What is this evil spirit? It is the spirit which would set itself up in the place of God. It would endeavour to demand man's total submission, claiming his body and soul as a master demands body and soul of his slave. It is the spirit of all that is evil – lying, hatred, deceit. It will deny both the almighty power of God and His loving care of all He has created. It would try to make this world alone the end of man and so would cast aside all those noble, inspiring ideas which come to everyone during their lifetime. This same spirit of materialism, of the denial of man's high destiny and of his soul and spirit, will reduce man to the position he occupied during those pagan days when Christ came to rescue the world.

Do you recall another visit of Our Lady to a child? It was at Lourdes when Mary appeared to Bernadette. What were Mary's words to that little child? Prayer and penance. Prayer, the loving communication between God and the creature which should be the mainspring and the force of every action of every day, and penance, the loving acceptance of the trials and sufferings which are the inevitable lot of man upon this earth.

This was, I have said, the message of Fatima, and it is the only solution to the problems which face us today. It is the only way by which man can be raised from the slough of despair and despondency and sense of frustration and which would, if left alone, envelop the human race. You have tried to appreciate this great truth. We want to win back the world to Christ and we want to do it God's way and not our own. Our divine Lord came to the world through a human mother and it is through that same mother that the world will return to Him.

Reproduced from *Westminster Cathedral Chronicle*.

Devotions and Hymns to Our Lady of Walsingham

Prayer for England

O Blessed Virgin Mary, Mother of God and our most gentle Queen and Mother, look down with mercy upon England thy Dowry, and upon us all who greatly hope and trust in thee. By thee it was that Jesus our saviour and our hope, was given unto the world; and he has given thee to us that we might hope still more. Plead for us thy children, whom thou didst receive and accept at the foot of the Cross, O sorrowful Mother! Intercede for our separated brethren, that with us in the one true fold they may be united to the Chief Shepherd, the Vicar of thy Son. Pray for us all dear Mother, that by faith fruitful in good works we may all deserve to see and praise God, together with thee, in our Heavenly home. Amen.

~~~

To the Blessed Virgin of Walsingham
(In the Celtic tradition) by John Rayne-Davis

Holy Mother of God and fount of wisdom, bless this sacred place of beauty and love. Here nature sings her praise to heaven in the swirling streams and the song of birds. Here lush flowers grow and hares play reflecting the glory of God. In this beautiful and holy place men and women through the ages have worshipped Christ and interceded His Blessed Mother and have come close to the Holy Spirit and Almighty God transforming their lives for ever.

~~~

Cardinal Mercier's Prayer to the Holy Spirit
(written from the Holy Ghost Chapel)

Holy Spirit, soul of my soul I adore you; enlighten, guide, strengthen and console me; tell me what I ought to do and command me to do it. I promise to be submissive in everything that you ask of me and to accept all that you permit to happen to me, only show me what is your will. Amen.

~~~

Ancient Walsingham Prayer written by Erasmus in 1511

O alone of all women, Mother and Virgin, Mother most happy, Virgin most pure, now we, sinful as we are, come to see thee who are all pure, we salute thee, we honour thee as how we may with our humble offerings; may thy Son grant us, that imitating thy most holy manners, we also, by the grace of the Holy Ghost may deserve spiritually to conceive the Lord Jesus in our inmost soul, and once conceived never to lose him. Amen.

~~~

Prayer to Our Lady of Walsingham

(From the *Pilgrim Manual* of the Anglican Shrine)

O Mary, recall the solemn moment when Jesus, your divine Son, dying on the cross confided us to your maternal care. You are our Mother; we desire ever to remain your devout children. Let us therefore feel the effects of your powerful intercession with Jesus Christ. Make your name again glorious in this place, once renowned throughout our land by your visits, favours and many miracles. Pray, O Holy Mother of God, for the conversion of England, restoration of the sick, consolation for the afflicted, repentance of sinners, peace to the departed. O blessed Mary, Mother of God, Our Lady of Walsingham, intercede for us. Amen.

~~~

Prayer for the Walsingham Association

God our Father, grant that we may do your will in all things. Fill us with the gifts of the Holy Spirit, so that receiving your Eternal Word with faith and holding Him fast in a good and honest heart, we may bear Him to the world with patience in all that we do and say. May we give due honour to Mary, His Mother, Our Lady of Walsingham, by imitating her life and thus encourage others of our generation to call her blessed. And may we come at last together with all members of the Association living and dead to the joys of eternal life. We ask this in the name of Jesus Christ our Lord who lives and reigns with you and the Holy Spirit, one God for ever and ever. Amen

Act of Entrustment to Our Lady of Walsingham, Mother of Vocation

(Community of Our Lady of Walsingham)

Hail, Mary, full of grace,
Holy Mary Mother of our Redeemer;
Mother of Vocation, Our Lady of Walsingham,
with great joy we call upon you.
Remember we are your children,
called to wholeness,
called to the fullness of joy,
called to realise our heart's deepest desire,
God's dream for us.
Woman of all graces,
woman of all Amens,
woman who followed him,
teach us to live always in the presence of God,
who wills us to become holy.
Sustain us, O Mother of Vocation
on our pilgrimage of faith;
help us to live the fullness of the call to life and love
wherever we find ourselves.
Guide us in making Spirit-filled choices,
so that your Immaculate Heart will triumph
and the Kingdom of God will come
in this land and throughout the world.
To you we entrust ourselves
and all peoples with our hopes and fears.
Joining our '*fiat*' to yours,
may our lives become a constant song of praise
and thanksgiving to God's glory.
O clement, O loving, O sweet Lady of Walsingham,

Mother of Vocation we trust in you.
Mother of England, of all nations and of all creation,
pray for us.
© COLW 2009

~~~

Our Lady of Walsingham

(From the Pynson Ballad, c.1465)

Walsingham, in thee is built 'New Nazareth'
Where shall be held in a memorial
The great joy of my salutation,
First of my joys, their foundation and origin
Root of mankind's gracious redemption,
When Gabriel gave me this news:
To be a Mother through humility
And God's Son conceive in virginity.
O England, you have great cause to be glad
For you are compared to the Promised Land, Zion
You are called in every realm and region
The Holy Land, Our Lady's Dowry.
In you is built new Nazareth,
A house to the honour of the Queen of Heaven
And her most glorious Salutation
When Gabriel said at Old Nazareth,
Ave, This same joy shall here be daily and for ever
remembered."

~~~

Walsingham Pilgrim Hymn

All Glory to God in His mercy and grace
Who hath stablished His home in this wonderful place.
Ave, Ave, Ave Maria! Ave, Ave, Ave Maria.

All Glory to Jesus our Saviour and Lord
Whose image within us by grace is restored.
Ave, ...

All Glory to God in His Spirit Divine
Who hath fixed His abode in this poor soul of mine.
Ave, ...

Sing the praises of Mary, the Mother of God
Whose 'Walsingham Way' countless pilgrims
have trod.
Ave, ...

Then lift high your voices, rehearse the glad tale
of our Lady's appearing in Stiflkey's fair vale.
Ave, ...

When Edward Confessor ruled over the land
The Faverche's Manor stood here nigh at hand.
Ave, ...

The Lady Richeldis devoted her care
to good works and penance and worship and prayer.
Ave, ...

One day as she prayed and looked up to the skies,
A vision of splendour delighted her eyes.
Ave, ...

Our Lady, God's Mother, in glory arrayed,
Held a house in her arms which was clearly displayed.
  Ave, ...

Take note my dear daughter, and build here a shrine,
As Nazareth's home in this country of thine.
  Ave, ...

And the spot that I choose where the house shall arise
By a sign shall be plainly revealed to your eyes.
  Ave, ...

The vision passed slowly away from her sight
But her mind held the house in its length, breadth
                                        and height.
  Ave, ...

Bewildered she pondered this message so sweet,
When a clear spring of water burst forth at her feet.
  Ave, ...

Bewildered no longer for this was the sign,
She vowed on this spot she would build such a shrine.
  Ave, ...

The finest materials her workmen could find
She employed for this house she had fixed in
                                        her mind.
  Ave, ...

But though she had given both timbets and lands,
The power of the work lay in Mary's own hands.
  Ave, ...

And this was made clear when the work was complete.
By the answers to prayers poured out at her feet.
  Ave, ...

And soon mighty wonders by Grace were revealed,
For the sick who made use of the waters were healed.
    Ave, ...

So Walsingham then came a place of great fame,
and Our Lady herself was called by this name.
    Ave, ...

And many a pilgrim to the day of his death,
Took the road once a year to England's Nazareth.
    Ave, ...

So crowded were roads that the stars, people say,
That shine in the heavens were called 'Walsingham
                                       Way'.

    Ave, ...

And many the favours and graces bestowed
On those, who in faith, took the pilgrimage road.
    Ave, ...

The image of Mary with her Holy Son
Was honoured and feted by everyone.
    Ave, ...

The Canons and Friars built houses around
And the praises of God were a regular sound.
    Ave, ...

And Kings, Lords and Commons their homage
                                     would pay
And the burning of tapers turned night into day.
    Ave, ...

But at last came a King who had greed in his eyes,
And he lusted for treasure with fraud and with lies.
    Ave, ...

The order went forth; and with horror 'twas learned.
That the shrine was destroyed and the image was
burned.
Ave, ...

And here where God's mother had once been
enthroned,
The souls that stayed faithful 'neath tyranny groaned.
Ave, ...

And this realm which had once been our Lady's
own Dower
Had its church now enslaved by the secular power.
Ave, ...

And so dark night fell on this glorious place
Where all former glories there hardly was trace.
Ave, ...

Yet a thin stream of pilgrims still walked the old way
And hearts longed to see this night turned into day.
Ave, ...

Till at last, when full measure of penance was poured,
In her Shrine see the honour of Mary restored.
Ave, ...

Again, 'neath her image the tapers shine fair
In her children's endeavours past wrongs to repair.
Ave, ...

Again in her house due honour is taught;
Her name is invoked, her fair graces besought.
Ave, ...

And the sick and the maimed seek the pilgrimage way,
And miraculous healing their bodies display.
Ave, ...

Oh, Mother give heed to the prayer of our heart,
that your glory from here never more may depart.
Ave, ...

Now to God the All-Father, and Son, with due praise,
And life giving Spirit, thanksgiving we raise.
Ave, ...

Bibliography

The Walsingham Story
   A. Bond. Privately published.
Message of Walsingham
   R.W. Connelly SM. Catholic Truth Society.
The History and Spirituality of Walsingham
   E.R. Obbard. Canterbury Press.
The Reformation in England
   Raymond Edwards. Catholic Truth Society.
The Handle and the Axe
   J.C.H. Aveling. Blond and Briggs.
The Roman Catholic Church in England and Wales
   E.E. Reynolds. Anthony Clarke.
Sixteenth Century England
   Joyce Yoings. Penguin Books.
The Tudors
   Christopher Morris. The Fontana Library.
Reformation 1490-1700
   D. MacCullogh. Penguin Books.
The Six Wives The Queens of Henry VIII
   David Starkey. Vintage Paperbacks.
The English Catholic Community 1570-1850
   John Bossy. Darton Longman & Todd.
Image and Devotion in Late Medieval England
   Richard Marks. Sutton Publishing, England.
The King's Reformation
   G.W. Bernard. Yale University Press.
The Black Death
   John Hatcher. Weidenfeld & Nicolson.